11. 50   TECH

D1643813

fibre to fabric

HAZEL KING

Heinemann
LIBRARY

www.heinemann.co.uk
Visit our website to find out more information about Heinemann Library books.

To order:
 Phone 44 (0) 1865 888066
 Send a fax to 44 (0) 1865 314091
Visit the Heinemann Bookshop at www.heinemann.co.uk to browse our catalogue
and order online.

First published in Great Britain by Heinemann Library,
Halley Court, Jordan Hill, Oxford OX2 8EJ,
a division of Reed Educational and Professional Publishing Ltd.
Heinemann is a registered trademark of Reed Educational & Professional Publishing Limited.

OXFORD MELBOURNE AUCKLAND
JOHANNESBURG BLANTYRE GABORONE
IBADAN PORTSMOUTH NH (USA) CHICAGO

Designed by AMR
Illustrations by Art Construction
Originated by Ambassador Litho Ltd
Printed in Hong Kong/China

ISBN 0 431 10560 X

04 03 02 01
10 9 8 7 6 5 4 3 2

British Library Cataloguing in Publication Data
King, Hazel
  Fibre to Fabric. – (Trends in textile technology)
  1.Textile fabrics – Juvenile literature 2.Textile fibres –
  Juvenile literature
  I.Title
  677

Acknowledgements
The Publishers would like to thank the following for permission to reproduce photographs:
Eye Ubiquitous, pp. 9, 14, 15; Gareth Boden, pp.22, 28, 31, 34, 40; Image Bank, p.21;
Photodisc, p.37; Science Photo Library, pp.4, 10, 12; Tencel ®, p.43.
Realia: DuPont (Tactel ®) p.20; The Woolmark Company p.31.

Cover photograph reproduced with permission of Tony Stone

Our thanks to Andy Rumsby for his comments in the preparation of this book.

Every effort has been made to contact copyright holders of any material reproduced in this book.
Any omissions will be rectified in subsequent printings if notice is given to the Publisher.

Any words appearing in the text in bold, **like this**, are explained in the glossary.

contents

the story of textiles

The term 'textiles' refers to any fabric or product made from fabric. A fabric product can be a piece of clothing, an accessory or a furnishing item. Furnishings are needed in the home, office, school, cinema, pub – even the car!

The production of textiles follows a very simple process:

fibre ➡ yarns ➡ fabrics ➡ fabric product

However, each part of this process has a chain of processes behind it! To fully understand the production of textiles it is necessary to start at the beginning. This means finding out about fibres.

Fibres

Fibres are the very basis of all fabrics. Fibres are used to produce **yarns** and yarns are used to make fabrics. The quality and **properties** of a fabric depend on the fibres from which it is made. All fibres can be described as being very fine, hair-like structures. They all have a similar characteristic, which is that they are very long in relation to their width. To understand this, look at your own hair. Even if it is short, a hair is many times longer than it is wide.

What are fibres?

All fibres are chemicals and are made up of large **molecules**. These molecules are known as **polymers**. Polymers have their atoms joined in long chains. This is what gives fibres their characteristic shape. In one single fibre there can be millions of molecules.

To be suitable for textiles, fibres must be strong and flexible. An item made of strong fibres performs well, whether it is a Lycra® top or a kitchen blind. Flexible fibres give a fabric its characteristic draping qualities, allowing it to hang, fold or gather.

Classifying fibres

Fibres come from a range of different sources. Believe it or not, they can be produced from plant seeds, plant stems, animal hair, crude oil, coal, trees, metals, minerals and caterpillars!

▼ *Magnified fibres: this is what the polyester fibre called Dacron® looks like when viewed under a microscope.*

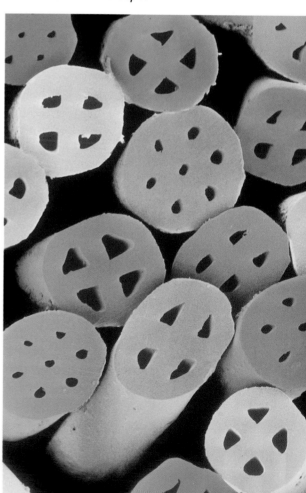

4

In order to make it easier to understand fibres, they are often grouped according to their place of origin. For example, some fibres come from a natural source. Others may be manufactured. Using these two general groups, fibres can then be classified further:

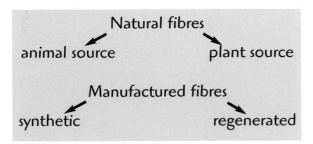

Natural fibres include all animal sources such as wool from sheep, silk from the silkworm and various animal hairs (camel, alpaca, angora etc). Plant sources of natural fibres include plants such as cotton, flax and jute.

Manufactured fibres are divided into those that are synthetic and those that are regenerated. Synthetic (chemically produced) fibres are usually made from crude oil and include nylon, polyester and acrylic. Regenerated fibres are a mixture of natural and synthetic sources. They include viscose, acetate and rayon.

New fibres and fabrics

Advances in technology mean that new sources for fibres are being investigated all the time. For example, one day you could be wearing clothes that have come from banana and pineapple leaves or the skin of salmon!

Today fabrics can be produced by combining several fibres together or by combining several layers of fabric. Very lightweight fabrics such as Lycra® are made using extremely thin, hair-like fibres known as microfibres.

The textile industry

The manufacture of textiles is usually divided into different areas. The fibre industry is responsible for the manufacture of fibres, the textile industry is responsible for the production of yarns and fabrics, and fabric products are made by the clothing or manufacturing industry. Together they make up the story of textiles.

▼ Fibre classification.

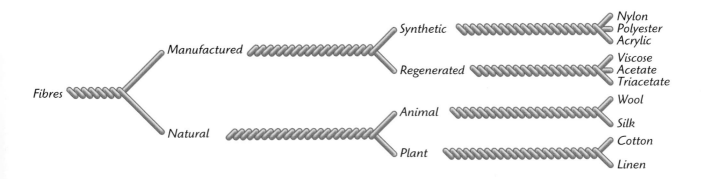

fibres around the world (1)

The production of commercial textiles is distributed fairly evenly throughout the Western world. Obviously manufactured fibres and fabrics can be made wherever there is access to raw materials and/or chemicals. However, as natural fibres originally come from plants or animals, their production tends to be restricted to areas where these are abundant. The geography of the main natural fibres is outlined here, along with some information about how these natural textiles begin their life.

Producing plant fibres

Like all plants, those that are used in the production of fibres require certain conditions for their growth. Great Britain, for example, is not hot enough for cotton plants to flourish, whereas Australia's climate is ideal. In 1999, Australia produced about 3 million **bales** of cotton and 95% of this was exported.

Cotton

Cotton grows on bushes and requires plenty of sunshine and moisture. Areas and countries with a warm, humid climate and good water supply include South America, South Africa, Argentina and India. However, altogether about 80 countries are involved in cotton production and the trade brings in a lot of money. Britain has to import its cotton from these countries. Just think about all the items that are made using cotton; from towels to bags and from lamp shades to vests!

Growing cotton

Cotton seeds are usually planted in the spring-time and develop into plants with creamy-white flowers. Gradually these flowers turn pink and then wither away, leaving behind a seed boll. Inside this boll seeds develop with long hairs attached. When the seeds reach maturity the boll bursts to reveal what looks like a fluffy ball of cotton wool.

Cotton fibres

One cotton boll contains thousands of fibres with an average length of 30mm. The bolls are collected from the plants either by hand or by machine. After harvesting, the fibres are separated from the seeds during a process known as ginning. There are two types of machine used for this process. The gin saw uses rotating blades to separate the fibres from the seeds and any impurities such as leaves or twigs. The roller gin has a revolving knife, set close to its surface, which scrapes away the seeds and impurities. The cotton fibres are then pressed into bales.

Cotton is graded according to its fibre length, colour and impurities. For example, Sea Island is a high quality cotton with fibres between 30mm and 65mm in length. On the other hand, Indian cotton has a fibre length of less than 20mm, giving it a coarser texture and lower grade.

Flax

The flax plant, *Linum usitatissimum*, grows in cool, damp climates with no extremes of temperature. About 20 countries grow flax, including Belgium, Russia, China, France and Ireland. Flax is used to produce the fabric we know as linen.

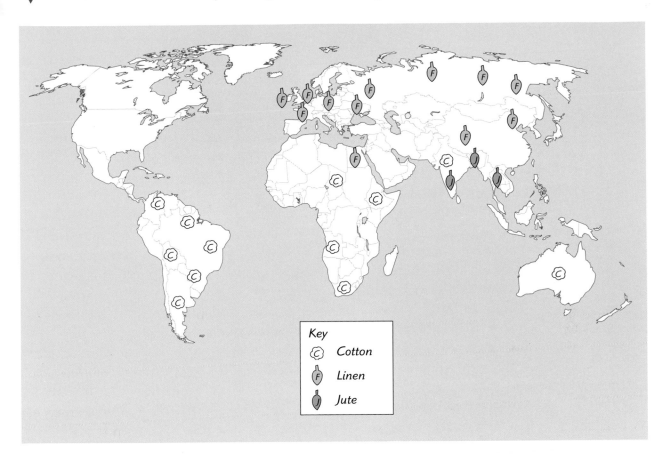

Flax was the first plant fibre to be woven, and linen was probably the first fabric to be made. It is known that Egyptian mummies were wrapped in linen cloth because, many thousands of years later, the cloth was found intact.

Growing flax
Flax plants have a single stem and grow to around one metre in height. They have blue and white flowers which grow at the top of the stem. After flowering, the plants are pulled up by their roots, just as the seeds are beginning to ripen. The stems are then left for several weeks while the dew, sun and rain bring about fermentation. This is known as retting and can be carried out more quickly using chemicals.

The stems (straw) are then passed through a breaking machine which separates the woody core from the flax fibres. The fibres are hackled (combed) to produce separate and parallel strands. The long fibres are used to produce fine **yarns** and the shorter ones produce coarser yarns of a lower quality.

Jute
Natural jute is yellowish-brown and has a silky texture. It is relatively inexpensive but is quite **labour-intensive** to produce. Jute plants need a damp climate, and grow from seed to about five metres in six months. The main jute-growing countries are Bangladesh, India and Thailand. Jute is used in the production of carpet-backing, packaging and clothing.

In the same way that plants require certain conditions for their growth, so animals need a particular climate and habitat. Animal fibres can be divided into three types: wool from sheep, silk from silkworms, and hair from goats, camels, rabbits, llamas and horses. The production of wool from sheep is a major part of the textile industry.

Wool

Many countries around the world produce wool, some of the main ones being Great Britain, Australia, New Zealand, South Africa and the United States. Different types and qualities of wool will have different end-uses and different breeds of sheep produce different types of wool. Wool may be divided simply into the following types:

- Coarse – the fibres are about 15cm long and are provided by Lincoln and Romney sheep. They may be used to make **worsted** fabrics.

- Medium – provided by Southdown and Corriedale sheep, the fibres are about 12–15cm long and have a slight **crimp**.
- Fine – these are the shortest fibres, about 5–12cm in length, and are highly crimped. They are provided by Merino and Ramboillet breeds of sheep.

Producing wool

The **fleece** is usually removed from sheep once a year. It is cut as a complete coat using power-operated clippers. The soiled edge around the fleece is removed and then it is graded and sewn into **bales**. The fleece is graded according to its colour, fineness, crimp, length of fibre and number of impurities. The bales are then sent to a mill for cleaning and **spinning**.

▼ *The main areas of the world producing wool, silk, cashmere and mohair.*

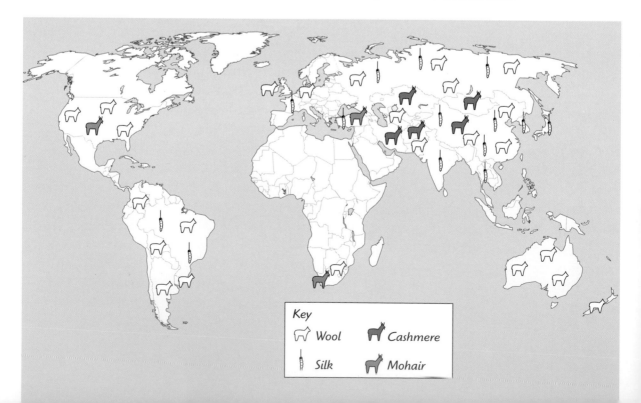

Key
- Wool
- Silk
- Cashmere
- Mohair

Camels provide us with two types of hair, from which we make blankets, ropes and warm jackets.

Silky productions

Silk fabrics often conjure up images of Eastern-style kimonos (Japanese garments) and this is not really surprising as silk has been produced in Japan and China for thousands of years. Both Japan and China still produce most of the world's silk, but they now have competition from India and Russia, with countries such as Thailand, Korea, Turkey, France and Brazil also manufacturing some silk. (The production of silk is explained in detail on pages 14-15.)

Animal hairs

Other animals, including goats, camels, rabbits, llamas and horses, provide the textile industry with more sources of natural fibres. These fibres are often used in knitwear and are expensive, mainly due to the fact that a large quantity is needed to produce just one textile item.

- The Tibetan Kashmir goat has an outer coat of long, coarse hair, but underneath this is a protected layer of fine, soft fibres. These are used to produce the extremely fine cashmere wool fibres used in garments such as coats and jackets.
- The Angoran goat provides mohair, a fibre often used in knitwear. Mohair fibres are long and accept dye easily; they have an attractive **lustre** and produce hard-wearing textiles. The best quality mohair comes from goats found in Texas (USA), South Africa and Turkey.
- Like the Kashmir goat the camel sheds two types of hair; the outer, coarse hairs are used to make blankets and ropes, while the softer, inner coat produces a warm fibre suitable for making suits and jackets.
- Not to be confused with the Angoran goat, rabbits produce a textile fibre known as angora. It is another long, soft fibre which gives a fluffy appearance to jumpers and cardigans.
- There are two types of llama bred for their hair – the alpaca and the guanaco. Llama fibres are mainly fine, soft and very warm and so tend to be used in high-quality knitted jackets, coats and blankets.
- Finally, horse hair is rarely used today as it is very rough, but in the past it was used as building material in walls, stuffing for furniture, and as a weighty material to hold down the hem of wedding dresses!

Cotton is a natural fibre because it comes from a plant source. During photosynthesis the cotton plant produces **cellulose** which is a **polymer** made from **glucose molecules** joined together. A cotton fibre contains millions of molecules of cellulose.

Cotton structure

The wall of the cotton fibre can vary in thickness but it is made up of two main sections: the primary wall and the secondary wall. In the centre of the fibre is a space known as the lumen. The primary wall is the tough, protective layer which contains cellulose, wax, protein and other substances. The secondary wall makes up the bulk of the fibre and is almost pure cellulose.

When the cotton fibre is growing on the plant its centre is filled with liquid nutrients so, at this stage, its cross-section is round. However, once the fibre dies the liquid disappears, leaving a space in the centre, the lumen. This explains the change in structure that occurs after cotton fibres are picked.

Twisted ribbons

As you can see in the photograph below, magnified cotton fibres look like twisted ribbons. The fibres actually grow as thin tubes, and it is only after they ripen that they take up this twisted state.

Processing cotton

When the cotton arrives at the **spinning** mill the **bales** are broken up to remove any seeds, leaves, twigs and dust. The fibres are loosened so impurities can be separated, and then they are blown against a perforated drum to remove any sand and grit. Further cleaning takes place as the cotton passes through a series of machines which continue to loosen the fibres by means of fans and beaters. The cotton finally emerges as soft, fleecy sheets known as laps. These huge rolls of cotton then go through three further processes: carding, drawing and spinning.

▼ *Cotton and polyester fibres, highly magnified. Cotton grows as thin tubes, but after ripening the tubes collapse into twisted ribbons. The cotton fibres are coloured green in the photograph.*

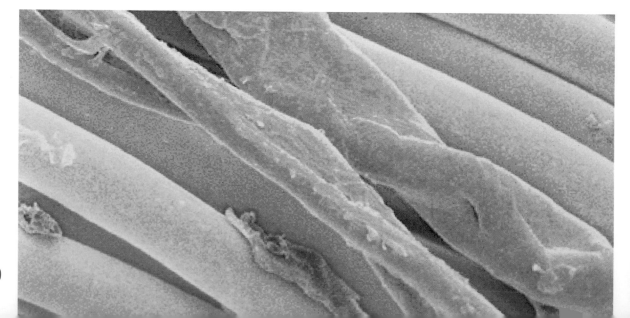

1 Carding

Carding machines 'open out' the laps using a sort of combing mechanism. This allows any short or immature fibres and impurities to be removed and results in a filmy web of cotton fibres. The fibres are then collected in a rope-like form known as a sliver.

2 Drawing

The slivers need to be made more uniform, and this is achieved by a series of rollers. As the cotton fibres pass through the rollers they become more closely aligned and 'drawn out' (hence the term 'drawing') so their thickness is reduced. The slivers are also combed again to get rid of any short fibres that remain, which might otherwise spoil the smooth surface of the finished **yarn**. The greater the number of drawing processes, the finer the yarn will be. After this drawing stage the cotton is known as roving.

3 Spinning

The spinning of cotton is based on a system known as ring spinning. The roving is fed from the rollers through a pot eye and twisted as it is wound on to the bobbin, which is rotating at high speed. Cotton is a strong fibre anyway so it is able to take a lot of twisting without breaking. The twist further improves its strength. The diagram below illustrates the technique which is used for most **staple fibre** yarns.

The ring spinning of cotton. This system of spinning was developed especially for cotton.

Mercerization

Cotton fibres are twisted in appearance, which is why cotton can lack **lustre**, or shine. However, cotton fibres have a hollow centre and this space can be used to produce a cotton fibre with greater lustre.

Mercerization is the process of treating cotton fibres with sodium hydroxide (caustic soda). The treatment causes the fibres to swell and untwist and so become smoother and rounder. Once the fibres have been rinsed the tension is released, producing a stronger, smoother fibre which is more absorbant and takes dye more easily.

This finishing technique is used on some sewing threads, which are labelled as 'mercerized cotton thread'.

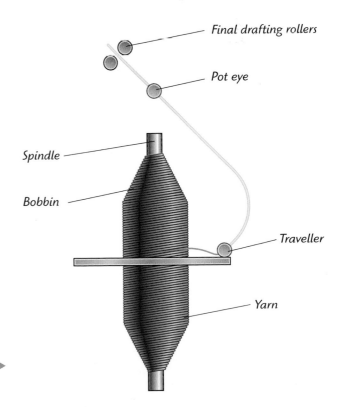

- Final drafting rollers
- Pot eye
- Spindle
- Bobbin
- Traveller
- Yarn

investigating fibres: wool

After cotton, wool is the second most widely used natural clothing fibre. It contributes softness, warmth, resilience and **drape** to textile products, although it is more specialized and restricted in its use than cotton.

Wool structure

Wool has a fascinating structure. If you look at wool fibres through a microscope you can see that they have a scaly appearance.

Wool fibres are made from a protein **polymer** which consists of **amino acids**. Wool protein has a complex structure consisting of about nineteen amino acids. The major protein in wool is keratin – the same protein found in the skin, hair and nails of human beings. There are three main parts to the wool fibre: an outer covering or epidermis, the central cortex, and an inner hollow core known as the medulla.

- The epidermis acts like a layer of wax to protect the fibre and repel water, although it does contain many microscopic pores which can absorb water vapour from the body. However, it is under this thin membrane that the irregular scales are found. They point towards the tip of the fibre and overlap one another to fit tightly together.
- The cortex gives the fibre its bulk. It consists of millions of spindle-shaped cells built up from **fibrils** and held together by a binding material. The structure of the cortex is what makes wool elastic (stretchy) and strong.
- The size of the medulla varies according to the type of wool fibre, with coarser fibres tending to have a larger hollow space.

▼ The scales on wool fibres. The fibres have a hollow centre around which there is a central cortex. The fibre is covered by an epidermis.

Wool crimp

Crimp is the name given to the permanent wave seen in wool fibres. This natural crimp is a significant feature of wool fibres, because it allows the fibres to stay together when twisted into a **yarn**. It also means that wool yarns can be very bulky and so are useful for making items which retain heat, such as blankets and sweaters. Fine wools are very crimpy but the crimp becomes less significant as the wool gets longer and coarser.

Processing wool

Wool fibres are much longer than cotton fibres although both are short and known as **staple** fibres. Long, highly crimped fibres are less easy to use with machinery than the shorter, straighter cotton fibres, so a more complicated set of processes is involved for wool.

1 Grading and sorting

Each **fleece** contains fibres of varying quality, so it must first be graded and sorted according to colour, fineness, crimp, length, and number of impurities.

2 Scouring

The wool cannot be processed further until its impurities have been removed, so the fleece is washed in large tanks of warm water and detergent. After three or four 'scourings' the wool is rinsed and dried. This process has to be carried out carefully to avoid tangling the fibres. The grease that is removed – lanolin – is sometimes used as an ingredient in the manufacture of cosmetics.

3 Carbonizing

Any remaining impurities are destroyed using highly acidic chemicals that 'eat' away the unwanted particles.

4 Carding

After going through the processes described above, the wool fibres need to be 'combed' to separate them. Carding machines carry out this task, producing a thin blanket of fibres ready for spinning.

5 Spinning

Wool may be spun into two types of yarn – woollen or **worsted** – depending on the type of fabric to be produced. These processes are outlined below.

Woollen yarns

Wool of shorter fibre length is the most commonly used, with only a limited amount of twist inserted in the yarn during spinning. The type of end-use for woollen yarns includes blankets, tweeds, coats and knitwear. The thin blanket of carded fibres are divided into 'slubbings', or ribbons, about 3cm in width. The slubbings are drawn out and spun, producing thick yarns with minimum twist.

Worsted yarns

These yarns are used for high-quality suits and other garments. After carding, the thin blanket of fibres is collected together to form a 'sliver' (a rope-like shape). Further combing is sometimes carried out to remove any short fibres and to ensure that the fibres are running parallel to each other. The fibres are then spun to produce a fine, firm, smooth yarn with a high degree of twist.

Over the years silk has been associated with many traditions and customs. Examples include silk wedding dresses, silk hoods worn during degree ceremonies, and lawyers who 'take silk' when they finally achieve the height of their profession. Today silk is still associated with wealth and luxury.

Silk filament

Silk is produced by the silkworm, which is the larvae of the silk moth – usually the *Bombyx mori* species. Unlike cotton or wool, silk fibres are **continuous filaments** rather than **staple** fibres. But, like wool they are made up of protein – mainly fibroin. However, the **amino acids** that make up their chemical structure and the way the amino acids are held together are quite different from wool, which explains why two protein fibres can produce such different end-products.

Silk **molecules** are closely packed together in some areas of the fibre and are more random in other areas. This produces a strong fibre but one that also has very little elasticity (stretchiness).

Natural silk

The silk moth lays eggs which take about three days to hatch. The new larva feed continuously on leaves of the mulberry tree. Within a month they reach maturity and start to spin their protective cocoon of fine, silk thread. The thread is a continuous filament, which the silkworm winds around itself hundreds of times.

The silkworm stores silk in liquid form in two glands and releases it through the exit hole in its head. One of the liquids is the protein fibroin and the other is a gum called sericin. As the silkworm spins the silk it is held together by the gum. First, the silkworm attaches the silk to a twig and then it gradually wraps itself in the continuous strand of silk by moving its head in a figure-of-eight motion. Eventually the silkworm changes into a chrysalis and finally hatches into a moth, which will emerge from the cocoon to lay more eggs and start the life cycle over again. When the moth is ready to leave the cocoon it secretes a substance which dissolves some of the silk, providing it with an escape hatch. This breaks the cocoon's threads, which means it is virtually useless in the production of silk.

Japanese girls dressed in silk for a special occasion. They are visiting a shrine in Kyoto.

Liquid silk is released from a hole in the silkworm's head. The cocoon is formed by moving the head in a figure-of-eight motion.

Sericulture

Commercial silk production is known as sericulture, and it is naturally centred in areas of Asia where mulberry trees are available. It normally involves killing the chrysalis before the moth has a chance to break free and destroy the silk cocoon. (The only exception to this is in the production of spun silk – see below.)

The eggs are spread out on trays containing mulberry leaves and are hatched by artificial warming. After the feeding process, the chrysalises are killed by subjecting the cocoons to either wet or dry heat. The cocoons are then soaked to soften the sticky gum and a revolving brush is used to find the ends of the filaments. A number of these filaments are drawn together through a guide and are given a slight twist to produce a **yarn** of the required thickness. This process is known as reeling and it produces threads of 'raw' silk.

Spinning silk

The **spinning** of silk is completely different from wool or cotton because the fibre is already continuous. When a manufacturer receives raw silk a process of throwing is usually applied. This is where two or three of the raw silk threads are twisted together to produce a silk yarn which can then be woven into fabric. The gum is often left on during these processes as it protects the silk fibres, but it needs to be removed later, at either the yarn or fabric stage of production. This de-gumming is carried out by boiling the silk with soap and water.

Types of silk

- Raw silk – creamy-coloured when it is untreated. It has a beautiful lustre owing to the way the filaments reflect light.
- Dupion silk – characterized by its uneven and thick appearance. Sometimes silkworms spin their cocoons together, producing 'double cocoons'. Dupion silk is produced by spinning the continuous filaments from these double cocoons at the same time.
- Tussah silk – produced by the uncultivated tussah moth, which lives on wild oak leaves. This silk is sometimes called 'wild silk' or tussore. It is a slightly coarser filament with a creamy colour and, as it does not take dye well, it is often left natural in colour. Another example of wild silk is shantung.
- Spun silk – a 'silkworm-friendly' silk! It is made from the staple fibres left after the moth has flown. These short silk fibres are known as noils and they have to be carded, combed and spun into yarns of silk. Many short fibres spun together do not produce as shiny a finish as a continuous filament. Consequently spun silk is not as lustrous or as expensive as silk from a continuous filament.

manufactured fibres

When textile technologists first started considering how to produce fibres, they used natural fibres as their starting point. Both cotton and linen fibres come from plants, and it was the cellulose found in plants which inspired the production of the first manufactured fibre.

Regenerated fibres

Towards the end of the nineteenth century, scientists began experiments to see whether wood could be used to produce new textile fibres. Wood is a good source of **cellulose** and trees could provide a plentiful supply. (Of course this was long before anyone was worried about using up the planet's natural resources!) The first manufactured fibre using cellulose from wood was known as rayon; today it is called viscose. The famous textile group Courtaulds eventually commercialized the viscose process in 1904.

So, first there were natural fibres and then fibres made from a natural source. The next step was to produce synthetic fibres ...

Synthetic fibres

Synthetic fibres were developed in America during the 1930s. DuPont, a huge chemical company, wanted to produce a substance that would make a suitable fibre for textiles. The basic substances had to be something they knew well, so they experimented with chemicals. These were obtained from oil, and then used to produce substances that could be spun. The end-product was nylon, or, as it is often called today, polyamide.

Although nylon became very popular during the 1950s and 1960s for clothes, household items and industry, by the mid-1970s its popularity was in decline. Today it is mainly used for stockings, tights, outdoor wear and carpets in the domestic market, although it is still used extensively in industry. It is one of the world's strongest fibres.

Complementing one another

Creating regenerated and synthetic fibres means that they can be produced virtually anywhere, rather than near areas where natural fibres are abundant, and they can be made to suit a particular purpose or function. Even better than that, natural and manufactured fibres can be blended so their specific characteristics can produce the ideal textile item. Aspects of one fibre can be complemented or enhanced by another fibre.

Manufactured fibres today

The production of all manufactured fibres follows the same basic principles. A fibre-forming substance is made liquid and then extruded – forced through tiny holes in a **spinneret** – after which the filaments are immediately made solid. However, as all fibres are different, the specific process they go through varies, as you can see from the diagrams opposite.

Extruding

The spinneret contains thousands of minute holes, or apertures. Obviously the shape of the holes will determine the shape of the fibre, and the shape of the fibre must be right for its end-use.

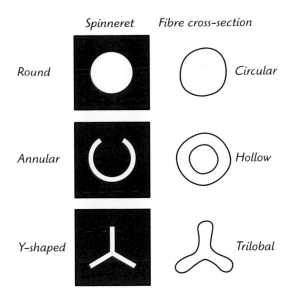

	Spinneret	Fibre cross-section	
Round			Circular
Annular			Hollow
Y-shaped			Trilobal

▲ Differently shaped spinnerets produce differently shaped fibres.

So, the holes are not always round. The diagram above illustrates some shapes that are commonly used. The annular shape produces circular fibres with a hollow centre. If polyester fibres are made this shape they have a bulky texture and are useful for wadding in jackets and duvets. The Y-shaped spinneret is used for carpets because the fibres do not show soiling to the same extent as circular fibres.

The liquid that is forced through the spinneret is known as a **polymer**, but once it has been extruded it is called a filament. These filaments are solidified and stretched to produce strong, uniform fibres that can then be twisted together to make either a continuous **yarn**, or **crimped** and cut to make shorter, **staple** lengths.

Spinning

Finally, the filament yarns are spun using one of three main methods:

- **Wet spinning** – polymer solution is pumped through a spinneret in a liquid bath; filaments are then drawn together and wound round a roller.
- **Dry spinning** – filaments are exposed to warm air to evaporate the solvents; then they are drawn together and wound round a roller.
- **Melt spinning** – polymer in a molten (melted) state is forced through the spinneret; the filaments are cooled by cold air before being drawn together and wound round a roller.

▼ The three main methods of spinning are known as wet, dry and melt spinning.

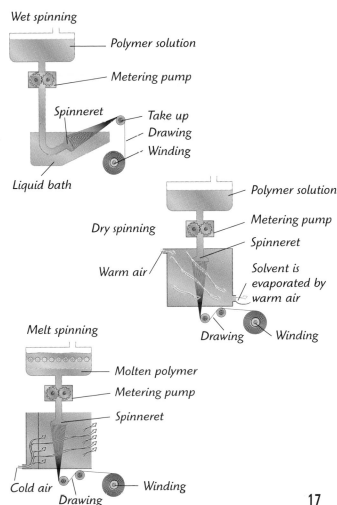

regenerated fibres

The term 'regenerated fibres' refers to fibres that have been produced industrially using natural **polymers**. Examples include viscose, modal, acetate, triacetate and Tencel®.

Copying silk

Although viscose was first produced commercially by Courtaulds in 1904, this was not the beginning of the story.

As early as 1664 an English scientist called Robert Hook predicted that it should be possible to produce fibres by simply copying silkworms and forcing a liquid through tiny holes.

Another two hundred years passed before the idea was successfully tried out by Louis Schwabe, an English weaver who melted glass and forced it through very fine holes. The glass solidified on cooling but it was a difficult fibre to process, so it was left to Sir Joseph Swan, in 1885, to produce the first 'artificial silk'.

Cellulose

Regenerated fibres are made from wood pulp which contains fibres of **cellulose**. Plants make about 50 billion tonnes of cellulose every year as part of the process of **photosynthesis**. In wood, the cellulose **molecules** are held together, but during processing the molecules can be rearranged into fibres.

Viscose

The wood used in the production of viscose is generally from spruce and eucalyptus trees. The bark is removed at pulp mills and the extracted cellulose is pressed and cut into sheets. These sheets are kept in conditions of controlled humidity and temperature until the moisture is evenly distributed.

The cellulose is then treated with sodium hydroxide (caustic soda) and carbon disulphide, dissolving it into a fluid. It ends up as a **viscous** solution of cellulose which can be forced through the tiny apertures in a **spinneret**.

The resulting filaments of pure cellulose are immersed in a bath of sulphuric acid, which breaks up the cellulose, neutralizes the sodium hydroxide and forms a viscose fibre. This is an example of **wet spinning** because the fibre is spun in sulphuric acid.

Although viscose is spun as a continuous filament it can be made into a **staple** fibre simply by chopping it up, which alters the characteristics of the end-product.

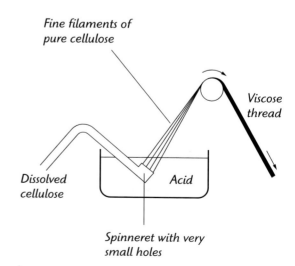

▲ Wet spinning cellulose. The solution is forced through very small holes into an acid bath, producing thin filaments of pure cellulose.

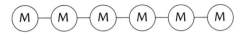
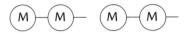
Modal

Viscose is no longer as popular as it used to be and an 'improved' viscose called modal has since been developed. It is made using a similar process but it is a stronger fibre which resembles cotton.

Acetate and triacetate

Acetate and triacetate, too, are made from wood pulp. In this case the cellulose is treated with acetic acid in a chemical process known as acetylation.

Unlike viscose, these regenerated fibres use the **dry spinning** method in their production, because the solvent used to dissolve the cellulose polymers is organic (formed from living things) and evaporates easily.

When the solution of polymer in the solvent is pumped through the spinneret into hot air, the solvent quickly evaporates at the holes of the spinneret, allowing fibres to form from the remaining polymers.

Acetate and triacetate have different **properties** from viscose, and are used only as filament **yarns**. Acetate has a look similar to that of silk and at one time it was known as 'artificial silk'. However, the name is no longer used in case people believe they are actually buying silk.

Tencel®

Tencel® is a regenerated cellulose-based fibre that was launched by Courtaulds in 1992. It causes less of an environmental impact than other regenerated fibres.

synthetic fibres

Synthetic fibres include polyamide, polyester, acrylic, elastane and aramids. They are made from **polymers** that have been produced artificially, although the starting point for the polymer is oil or coal.

Making polymers

The process of making polymers is known as **polymerization**. This simply means the adding together of smaller **molecules** to produce a larger molecule (or polymer). There are three methods of polymerization used to make textile materials:

* Polymerization, e.g. acrylic – similar **monomers** are added to one another ○-○-○-○-○-○-
* Condensation polymerization, e.g. polyamide – two different monomers react together -○-□-○-□-○-
* Copolymerization, e.g. stretchy nylon – if two or more different monomers are polymerized together this produces a copolymer. These can be designed to have specific **properties** -○-□-◇-○-□-◇-.

Polyamide

Nylon is an example of a polyamide fibre, and Tactel® is a brand name for one type of polyamide. The scientist Wallace H. Carothers, who worked at DuPont in America, takes the credit for the discovery of nylon, using coal. He also developed **melt spinning** and a synthetic rubber known as neoprene.

The original method of producing nylon involved the joining of two chemicals to form a nylon polymer. It was called nylon 6.6 to reflect the arrangement of atoms in the molecule. Another method of making nylon was developed later and this time only one substance was used during polymerization. The new nylon was called nylon 6. As far as the consumer is concerned, fabrics made using these two methods are identical as they behave in the same way in clothes and household items. Today nylon is usually produced using oil rather than coal as the starting point.

Tactel® is a registered trademark of DuPont.

Only by DuPont

Polyester

As a result of the discoveries made by Carothers, two scientists working for Calico Printers Association in Britain went on to develop some new polyester fibres. Eventually a polyester called Terylene® was produced by ICI, and later in America a polyester based on the same polymer was produced by DuPont, called Dacron®.

Producing polyester

Today polyester is made worldwide and is regarded as one of the most important textile fibres. It is used in the production of a whole range of products, both domestic and industrial. The raw material for polyester is oil, which is used to make a substance that can be polymerized.

Polymerization takes place and the polymer is extruded, cut into chips and dried. Unlike viscose and acetate, polyester is spun without any solvents. The polymer is melted and pumped through a spinneret; then, as it meets the cold air it solidifies forming a fibre. This method is known as melt spinning. Polyester can be produced as both a filament and a fibre, depending on its end-use. Staple fibres have to be **crimped**, heat set and cut after the spinning process.

Acrylic

Acrylic fibres are based on a polymer called polyacrylonitrile. During production wet or dry spinning are used because they do not involve high temperatures. The acrylic polymer would break down in the presence of heat. 'Acrylic' is the **generic** name for fibres manufactured from at least 85% polyacrylonitrile. The remaining 15% can come from other monomers which means many variations are possible.

Familiar brand names for acrylic include Courtelle® and Dralon®.

Elastane

Elastane is a fibre that has the ability to stretch and recover – over 500%! This feature has enabled the clothing industry to produce a wealth of figure-hugging garments. It is a complicated substance made initially from oil, and it is often blended with other fibres. Brand names include DuPont's Lycra®.

Aramids

This group of fibres is particularly important in the production of fire-resistant materials. The fibres are very strong and have a high melting point. However, if they do catch fire they self-extinguish once the source of heat has been removed. Examples of items made from aramid fibres include high-pressure hoses, foundry gloves, and suits for racing drivers.

Many people rely very heavily on the performance of textile items, particularly for safety reasons. Tough and durable garments are often needed in the workplace.

the properties of fibres

All fibres have specific characteristics or **properties** that make every fibre unique. When a fibre is spun into a **yarn** its properties are improved. For example, many hard-wearing or **durable** fibres spun together make a more durable yarn, and once the yarn becomes a fabric it is even more hard-wearing.

Properties of a fibre include strength, stretch elasticity, durability, warmth, water absorbancy, resistance to micro-organisms and insects, crease recovery, flammability and chemical resistance.

Measuring properties

Many of the properties associated with fibres are measurable. In other words, tests can be carried out to determine how much of a certain property a fibre has. For example, the strength of a fibre is measured by testing its **tenacity**. This refers to the degree of resistance to breaking that a fibre has when force is applied.

However, there are some properties that cannot easily be measured with tests. These relate to **aesthetic** and **tactile** qualities – the look and feel of a fabric – and are known as design attributes. They tend to be more subjective. For instance, some people may not enjoy the hairy feel of wool once it has been made into a fabric and would rather have the smooth texture of silk next to their skin.

Some of the properties of different fibres are outlined here.

Strength, stretch and elasticity

As has been mentioned, the strength of a fibre is measured by its tenacity. This can be defined as the breaking force per unit of fineness. In this case, fineness refers to the size of the cross-section of a fibre. The degree to which a fabric can withstand the breaking force is known as its **tensile strength**. This property is important when the end-use is dependent upon strength, for example, a polyamide seat belt in a car.

On the other hand, the degree to which a fibre stretches is known as its **extensibility** and is caused by the **molecules** slipping as the pressure is applied to the fibre. It is usually written as a percentage of the original length. The extensibility of polyester, for example, is between 15% and 50%.

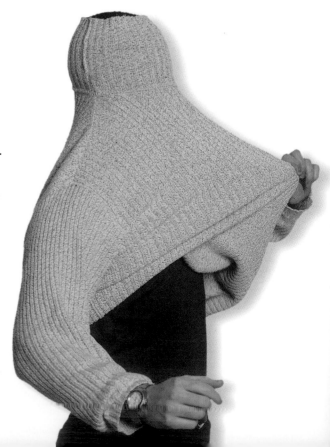

All fibres have specific properties. Wool is a very stretchy fibre which makes it ideal for garments such as jumpers.

Elastic recovery

An elastic fibre is important for the production of products that must stretch and return to their original shape. A jumper is a good example of this as it needs to stretch as you put it on but return to its size and shape once you are wearing it. If a fibre is stretched by a small amount and returns to its original length when released, it is said to have an elastic recovery of 100%.

Crease recovery

Just as a fibre may recover completely after being stretched, it may also return to its original shape after being creased. Many textile items are enhanced or made more convenient through the crease recovery of their fibres. Manufactured fibres such as polyamides and polyesters have good crease recovery properties, although crease-resistant finishes are available today.

Warmth

Clothes and other items that are designed to keep us warm rely on the ability of the fibres to trap air within the yarns and within the fabric. It is not that some fibres are 'warmer' than others but that some fibres trap more air than others. Hairy fibres like wool are able to hold air much more efficiently than the smooth fibres of viscose. The insulating effect of air helps us to stay warm – which is why wearing layers of thin clothes is better than wearing one thick layer.

Water absorbancy

A fibre's ability to absorb moisture is known as its moisture regain. This is the weight of absorbed water written as a percentage of the dry weight of the fabric. Fibres may need to absorb perspiration, moisture from the atmosphere, rain, spillages etc. A fibre's ability to absorb moisture will also influence how easy it is to clean.

Properties of fibres

A summary of the main properties of some fibres are shown here using a rating scale of 0–10, where 0 is low and 10 is high

Property	Cotton	Wool	Flax	Silk	Viscose	Polyester	Nylon	Elastane
Strength	8	1	10	8	5	10	10	5
Elasticity	8	10	0	8	1	8	10	10
Durability	10	1	10	10	1	10	10	10
Crease recovery	1	10	0	5	1	10	8	10
Warmth	5	10	5	8	0	1	0	1
Water absorbancy	10	10	10	10	10	0	0	1

comparing fibres

Cotton

Cotton is an incredibly versatile fibre and can be used to make many different fabrics and end-products. Its most important **property** is its ability to absorb moisture. Sports tops are often made from cotton because the fibres are able to absorb perspiration and then allow it to evaporate. This means the moisture in the fibres quickly vaporizes and the wet cotton top does not cling to the person wearing it. This is why cotton clothes usually feel comfortable.

Cotton is a strong fibre, and can be used for a whole range of items. It is actually stronger when wet, so most cotton items can be washed regularly. Cotton fibres readily absorb water so they are also easy to keep clean. Although cotton fibres dry easily, they do not resist creasing very well.

Wool

Wool is warm because its fibres are efficient at trapping air. However, there are many different types of wool and different methods of **spinning** them, so wool fibres have a variety of end-uses. Some wool fibres are finer and straighter than others which means they are not as good at trapping air as the thicker, hairy types. Many wool fibres also have the tactile quality of softness.

Wool's special property is its ability to absorb moisture. It can absorb up to one third of its weight in moisture before it even feels wet. This great absorbancy is what makes wool products so heavy when they are being washed.

Unfortunately, wool does not dry very quickly and can easily stretch out of shape when wet.

Wool fibres have a unique **crimped** shape which contributes to the property of elasticity. When stretched a wool fibre will naturally spring back to its original shape; therefore the crease recovery of wool is good and it also 'hangs' well.

Flax

The properties of the fabric linen are provided by flax fibres. Flax has great moisture absorbancy and so, like cotton, it is cool to wear in a hot climate. It absorbs perspiration and allows it to evaporate quickly. It is also a strong and hard-wearing fibre, although it creases badly owing to its low **extensibility** and elasticity.

Silk

Although silk fibres are not hairy and do not trap air in the same way as wool, they can produce fabrics with insulating properties. This is because the fibres are so fine and smooth that the resulting fabrics can be tightly woven. A silk garment, such as a shirt, traps body heat under the fabric and keeps the body warm. Like wool, silk can absorb one third of its weight in moisture before it feels wet, although perspiration and other chemicals can cause a change in its colour.

The **aesthetic** qualities of silk are very important to many people. Its extremely smooth texture has made it a popular choice of fibre for the production of underwear and nightwear.

Viscose

Viscose fibres are strong, although they are not as strong as cotton and they become less strong when wet. Their strength is mainly due to good extensibility. The elasticity of viscose is low, so it has poor crease recovery. It also lacks insulating properties because the smooth fibres do not trap air. However, viscose absorbs moisture well.

Polyester and polyamide

These fibres have similar properties as both are synthetic. In the production of manufactured fibres, desired qualities can be introduced rather than relying on what nature can provide. Both polyester and polyamide are very strong fibres with high **tenacity**, which also means they are very **durable**. They both have good elasticity and therefore good crease recovery. Moisture absorbancy is poor for these fibres, which is why they are often used as a blend in many items of clothing, e.g. cotton/polyester blend.

Elastane

Elastane is a unique manufactured fibre with tremendous elasticity. One of the brand names for elastane is Lycra®, which is probably more familiar to most people. It is used in products that require a great deal of stretch but also need to recover fully. Like the other synthetic fibres it has high durability and crease recovery (see 'Properties of fibres' table on page 23).

Properties and end products

Fibre	Main properties	Suggested end-products
Cotton	water absorbancy, durability	towels, tea towels, underwear, shirts, baby clothes
Wool	warmth, elasticity, crease recovery, water absorbancy	jumpers, blankets, carpets, bags, suits, dresses
Linen	durability, water absorbancy, strength	shirts, skirts, trousers, tops, dresses, curtains
Silk	durability, water absorbancy	cushions, wall hangings, shirts dresses, underwear, bedclothes
Viscose	flammability, water absorbancy	linings for jackets and coats, curtains, trousers
Polyester	durability, strength, crease recovery	car seat covers, rugs, curtains, pleated skirts, suits
Nylon	durability, strength, elasticity	carpets, jackets, coats, umbrellas, tents, ropes bedclothes
Elastane	durability, elasticity, crease recovery	sportswear, leggings, vest tops, jeans

identifying fibres

Sometimes you need to be able to identify the type of fibre a fabric sample contains. If you have a fabric for a textile product and the fibre content is unknown, it may be unsuitable for the specific end-use of that product.

Obviously if the fabric is made from a blend of fibres it is more difficult to discover what the fibres are. It requires careful, step-by-step testing. Some of the tests that can be used to identify fibres are explained here, although they would need to be carried out in suitable conditions and under supervision.

Can't stand the heat?

Some fibres burn more readily than others and they also react differently while they are burning. Testing a fibre's flammability is often carried out in two stages. First, the fibre sample is placed close to, but not in, the flame to see whether or not it is **thermoplastic**. A thermoplastic fibre softens and melts at high temperatures rather than burns, so it is likely to shrink away from the flame or melt into a bead.

Then the sample is placed in the flame to observe its reaction. A number of reactions can occur: the fibres may or may not burn; smoke may be produced; there may be a smell; the fibre may burn slowly or quickly; there may be a residue of ash. All reactions need to be carefully noted if an accurate identification is to be made. The following table is a guide to possible observations when different fibres are burnt.

Fibre	Observations of flame test	Thermoplastic
Cotton	Burns rapidly with a clear flame, leaves a powdery ash; ash smells of burnt paper	No
Wool	Quickly goes out and smells like burning hair	No
Linen	Similar to cotton; burns with clear flame and leaves a powdery ash	No
Silk	Does not burn readily; smells like burning hair	No
Polyamide	Burns slowly; leaves drops of molten polymer; smoky flame	Yes
Acrylic	Burns with a smoky flame and drops molten polymer	Yes
Polyester	Produces molten beads of polymer as it slowly burns; leaves behind hard beads	Yes
Viscose	Burns rapidly with a clear flame; leaves a black ash that is slightly sticky	No

Under the microscope

As we have seen, different fibres have different lengths and their cross-section can have different shapes. So, by studying fibres under a microscope, we can make an identification according to their appearance.

To look at the length or longitudinal view of the fibres, separate them from one another and place them on a microscope slide, suitably mounted and covered with a cover slip. The best general-purpose magnification to use is 100 times.

Looking at the cross-section of fibres is a little more tricky but one of the simplest ways is to use a thin stainless steel plate that has a small hole in it. Fold a thread of sewing cotton in half and push the fold through the hole in the metal plate. This creates a loop under which the fibres can be placed. Gently pull the sewing thread back until the hole is filled with fibres. Cut the fibres to form a 'tuft' on the top of the plate and then mount and cover them so they are secure. The magnified fibres can be observed and compared with diagrams such as the ones shown here.

Chemical analysis

Finally, some fibres can be identified by testing for the presence of chemicals in their structure. These tests are usually carried out on thermoplastic fibres.

The nitrogen test involves placing some fibres in a tube and covering them with soda lime. The tube is heated using a bunsen burner flame until the fibres decompose. The decomposed matter is then tested with red litmus paper. If the paper turns blue, nitrogen is present, which means the fibre is likely to be a polyamide or an acrylic.

In the chlorine test, fibres are placed on a copper wire which is heated to a high temperature in a bunsen burner flame. If a green colour shows in the flame, the fibre is likely to be a type of acrylic.

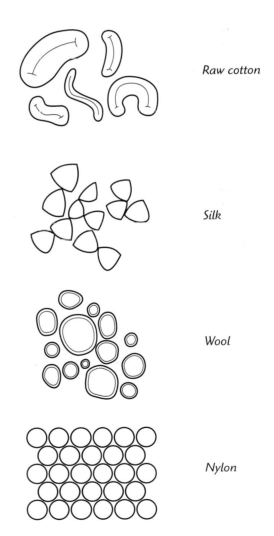

Raw cotton

Silk

Wool

Nylon

▲ Magnified fibres. The cross-sections of different fibres can help with identification.

blending fibres

Every fibre has its own special **properties** and characteristics. However, no single fibre has all the desired properties for a particular outcome. So, by combining fibres the best properties of both fibres can be exploited. At the same time, the less desirable qualities of one fibre can be balanced out by another. Textile items have been improved in this way for many years. One of the earliest examples was a blend of wool and cotton. Viyella® is the brand name of a fabric containing 55% wool and 45% cotton.

Blend together

Blending different fibres is useful because it not only improves their overall properties but also increases the range of **yarns** and fabrics available. A blend of expensive, natural fibres with less expensive, manufactured fibres will produce a more economical end-product. A mix of absorbant cotton fibres and less absorbant polyester fibres provides textile items that are more practical for the consumer. For even greater variation, several different fibres can be used to produce blended yarns and fabrics.

Dyeing to be different

The ability to absorb dye is another characteristic of fibres. Different fibres have different **affinities** for the various dyestuffs available. Cross-dying takes place after a fabric has been made, so if more than one type of fibre has been used, the end result will be a fabric of varying shades of colour. A fabric can be woven in such a way that once it has

been dyed a particular pattern or design can be achieved. Examples are checks, stripes and plaids.

▼ *Fabrics can be woven into a vast selection of patterns and designs.*

Blend or mix?

Most fabrics containing two or more fibres are known as a blend. During weaving, one type of fibre may be used in the **weft** and another in the **warp**, so achieving yet another effect. However, if two or more different yarns are used which contain different fibres, and these yarns are woven or knitted together, the resulting fabric is called a mix or mixture.

How much is enough?

It is not only the type of fibres that are blended together that determines the overall properties of a fabric, but also the amount used of each. The fibre in the greatest quantity is likely to be the one whose properties dominate the blend. A shirt that contains just 10% silk will not feel very silky. However, that is not to say that all blends should be 50:50; it all depends on the characteristics required for its end-use. The label shown here is for some easy-care (washable) trousers that have some stretch but do not lose their shape.

▼ *A wash care label.*

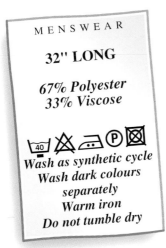

MENSWEAR

32" LONG

67% Polyester
33% Viscose

Wash as synthetic cycle
Wash dark colours
separately
Warm iron
Do not tumble dry

Choosing fibres

The choice of fibres to be blended together will very much depend on the end-use. Very often blends contain both natural and manufactured fibres because they can contribute different properties to the end-product. The desirable qualities of an everyday garment such as a shirt might include comfort, durability, easy-care and strength. A natural fibre such as cotton would provide the comfort, strength and easy-to-wash qualites, while polyester would contribute durability and easy-care properties.

The advantage of using manufactured fibres in the blending process is that many of them can be produced to the specific length and fineness required for a particular end-use.

A popular choice

Many fabrics use polyester as part of their blend. This is because polyester is a strong, durable fibre with good crease-resistance and, when blended with a more **aesthetically** pleasing fibre, the overall performance is high. Examples of these blends include polyester/cotton, polyester/viscose and wool/polyester.

Benefits of blending

Blending fibres is clearly of benefit to both the consumer and the manufacturer. The benefits include:

- a wider variety of yarns and fabrics

- an improvement in the overall properties and performance

- enhanced aesthetic qualities

- cheaply produced (and therefore less expensively priced) textile items.

spinning a yarn

Making textiles is one of the oldest crafts we know of. Prehistoric people used animal skins as a form of clothing and bedding. Matted **fleece** from sheep was the earliest form of felt, and eventually a type of fabric was made by twisting together fibres from a fleece, then weaving them to produce a piece of material. The same principle was later applied to other natural fibres – linen, cotton and silk.

Give it a twist

So far we have seen how fibres can be produced from natural, regenerated and synthetic sources. These fibres may be one of two types, **staple** or continuous. As they are, staple fibres are too short to be useful for fabric production, and all fibres are generally too thin and fragile to be made into textile items on their own. So, the next step is to produce **yarns** from the fibres.

Spinning is a process of twisting which adds strength and volume to fibres. Different amounts of twist can be applied to the fibres. For example, a loose twist will produce a soft, bulky yarn whereas a tight twist will produce a stronger, finer yarn. A loose twist will be required in a yarn that is to be woven into a fabric suitable for an item that must **drape** well, such as a pair of trousers. If drape is not important, a tightly twisted yarn is possible.

Twisting right

A twist can be applied to fibres in one of two ways; to the right or to the left. (In other words, clockwise or anti-clockwise.)

This has an effect on the end-result, and yarns can be defined according to the type of twist they have been given. Twisting to the right (clockwise) produces a yarn with fibres flowing in the same way as the letter S. Unsurprisingly, this is known as an S-twist. Fibres that are twisted in an anti-clockwise direction follow the direction of the letter Z. So, this is called a Z-twist. Both twists are illustrated in the diagram below.

▼ An S-twist goes the same way as the letter S. A Z-twist goes the same way as the letter Z.

Applying the yarn

Spinning fibres together to bind them produces a single yarn. However, yarns themselves can be twisted together to form plied yarns. The more single yarns used, the greater the strength and volume of the final yarn and fabric. It is important that the yarns are twisted in the opposite direction to the original twist of the fibres, otherwise the yarn could untwist and knot up. When two yarns are twisted together, the yarn is called two-ply, three yarns make a three-ply yarn, and so on. This 'ply' system (shown opposite) is clearly illustrated in the labelling of knitting wools.

Spinning jenny

Today's various spinning processes are fast and highly productive. However, spinning was initially carried out by hand and then using a spindle. By 1765 the first electrically powered spinning machine was invented in Britain. James Hargreaves called his invention the spinning jenny. This revolutionized the spinning process by allowing many threads to be spun at the same time. This was really a response to the invention of the flying shuttle, which greatly improved and speeded up the process of weaving. If weaving could be done more quickly, spinning had to catch up! Even before the introduction of the flying shuttle, it took five spinners to keep one weaver supplied with yarn.

▲ Yarns spun into a great assortment of colours and textures.

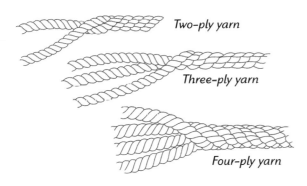

Two-ply yarn

Three-ply yarn

Four-ply yarn

◄ The ply system. Yarns are twisted to produce two-, three- and four-ply yarns.

▼ The Woolmark is given only to items made from Pure New Wool.

CERTIFICATION TRADE MARK

WOOLMARK

The Woolmark logo is a Registered Trade Mark owned and controlled by The Woolmark Company

A look back in time

You can visit working mills today to see how textiles used to be produced. For example, Quarry Bank Mill in Cheshire is Europe's largest working museum of the cotton industry. Ex-mill workers demonstrate the production of cotton, from fibre to fabric, just as it would have been produced after the **Industrial Revolution**.

textured yarns

Manufactured **yarns** are produced as **continuous filaments**, and this means they are very good at producing fabrics with a thin, flat and shiny surface. However, such fabrics have limited use. Since the 1950s, textile technologists have been working on ways to add bulk and texture to manufactured fibres.

Chop it up

It is possible to copy naturally bulkier fibres such as linen, wool and cotton by chopping up the continuous filament to create **staple** fibres. These are then spun in the usual way to give a bulkier yarn. However, this process is relatively expensive in terms of both time and money, and it seems wasteful to cut up a perfectly good continuous filament. The desired effect has to be achieved using a filament instead of a staple.

Texturing

Texturing is the process of adding bulk to continuous filaments. There are a variety of techniques available and they all rely on the premise that a **crimped** yarn has more bulk than a straight one. Continuous filaments are made up of thinner filaments called monofilaments. If each monofilament is crimped, the finished yarn is bulkier and stretchier. As heat is applied to 'fix' the crimp, **thermoplastic** filaments have to be used. The main methods of adding a false crimp to filaments are outlined here:
- **False-twist** – in this process the manufactured yarn is twisted and heat set in the twisted position. Then, it is twisted in the opposite direction, which partially untwists the yarn.

False-twist nylon and polyester yarns are often used in stockings, tights, ski-pants, gloves and swimsuits.

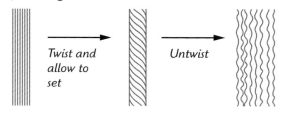

▲ False-twist adds texture to yarns.

- **Air bulking** – this is used on polyamides in the production of Tactel®. Heated yarns are passed through jets of air which blow little loops and crimps into the filaments. Although the result is a bulkier yarn, it tends not to be as stretchy as false-twist yarns and so is used in woven fabrics.

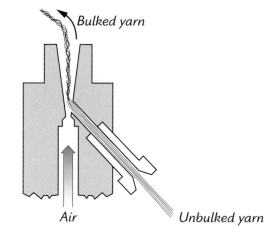

▲ Air bulking is used in the production of Tactel®.

- **Stuffer-box crimping** – as its name suggests, this method involves stuffing a yarn into a box. The filaments are folded in a zigzag fashion into a heated box and, due to the heat, the yarn retains its shape.

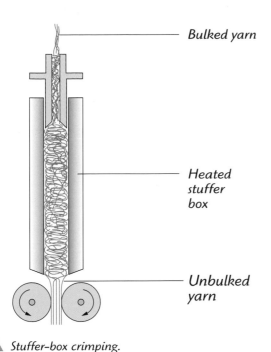

Bulked yarn

Heated stuffer box

Unbulked yarn

▲ Stuffer-box crimping.

- **Knife-edge crimping** – this applies the same principle as curling paper by pulling it over the edge of a scissor blade. Once again, the yarn is heated and then passes via rollers over the edge of a knife, adding waves and crimps to the finished yarn.

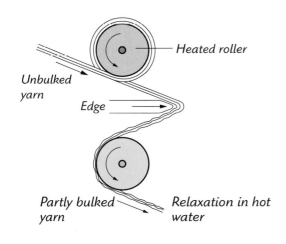

Heated roller

Unbulked yarn

Edge

Partly bulked yarn

Relaxation in hot water

▲ Knife-edge crimping.

Fancy that

Fancy or novelty yarns can be produced by varying the spinning technique. For example, by **spinning** together yarns of different type or colour, or by altering the amount of twist, a whole variety of effects can be achieved. Fancy yarns are usually made from more than one yarn, and one of the plies used is regarded as the core ply.

- A bouclé yarn is an uneven, loopy yarn. Any item made from it will also end up with this loopy effect. It is made using three yarns. One acts as the core ply, the second twists around the core, and the third, which is fed in at a faster rate, produces the loops.
- Knop contains knots or twists. It is also made from three plies, and special spinning adds little twists at intervals, creating a knot effect.

Slub fabrics

Coarse, less expensive linen or silk may have occasional uneven threads, and manufacturers have tried to recreate this effect in some of their fancy yarns. The term 'slub' refers to yarns and fabrics with this uneven texture.

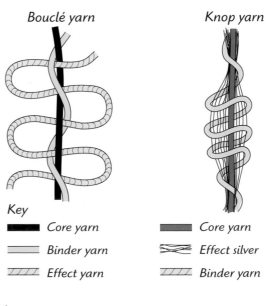

Bouclé yarn

Knop yarn

Key

▬▬ Core yarn

▭ Binder yarn

▱▱▱ Effect yarn

▬▬ Core yarn

⨯⨯ Effect silver

▱▱▱ Binder yarn

▲ Fancy yarns.

making fabrics

Once a **yarn** has been created it can be used to produce a fabric. Traditionally there were just two ways of doing this: weaving and knitting. However, technology has improved this situation and fabrics can be produced using a variety of means. The different processes may be divided up as follows:
- Fabrics made using fibres directly, e.g. felt or bonded materials
- Fabrics made using yarns, e.g. weaving, knitting, braiding and open-work
- Fabrics made using a combination of the above, e.g. laminated fabrics.

Fabrics from fibres

Obviously it would be very difficult to weave fibres together, so non-woven fabrics are produced by matting and bonding the fibres. Felt is a non-woven fabric usually made from wool, although other animal hairs may be used, such as camel, rabbit or goat. If woollen garments are not washed carefully the fibres are said to 'matt' or 'felt', and this is the principle upon which felt is based. Felt has some of wool's **properties**; for example, it is a good insulator and absorbs water well. However, as a fabric it is fairly stiff and does not **drape** well, so felt's main uses are not in the area of clothing (with the exception perhaps of hats) but in more unusual items, such as protective layers under ornaments, coverings for snooker tables, baby toys and pin cushions.

Bonded fabrics are those produced by adhering fibres together. This may be done by needle punching, stitch bonding, thermal bonding or adhesive bonding. These fabrics are important because they are quicker and less **labour-intensive** than the more conventional methods of fabric production. Bonded fabrics have a wide range of applications both domestically and commercially. Disposable items of fashion clothing never really took off (despite the introduction of throw-away knickers in the 1960s!), but the need for disposable gowns and masks in the medical world has made excellent use of bonded fabrics. Also, such diverse items as J-cloths and Vilene (an **interliner**) are made from bonded materials.

Fabrics from yarns

In order to produce a fabric, yarns need to be held together without losing their softness or flexibility. The main ways of achieving this are through weaving and knitting and, although today's methods involve high-speed, computer-controlled machines, the principles of these ancient techniques remain the same.

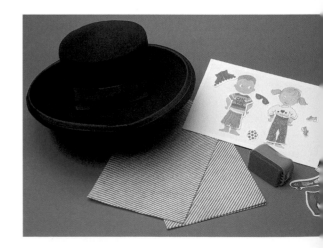

▲ *Felt and bonded fabrics are used to produce a wide range of textile items.*

Weaving is the interlacing of yarns at right angles to one another. The fabric is held together by the friction created at the points where the yarns cross. The edges of the fabric form a **selvedge** which stops the sides from fraying. A woven fabric is made from two types of yarn, those which run the length of the fabric, in the direction of the **warp** (ends), and those running the width of the fabric, in the direction of the **weft** (picks). The way in which these yarns are woven together forms the type of weave for that particular fabric. For instance, a simple plain weave is produced when the picks are laced over one end and under the next. Other types of common weave include twill and satin.

Weft direction

Pick   End   Selvedge

Warp direction

▲ Weaving is the interlacing of yarns at right angles.

The second main way of holding yarns together is knitting, which forms a fabric by interlocking loops of one yarn. Hand knitting is carried out with the aid of knitting needles, and the yarn is introduced across the fabric; so hand knitting is known as weft knitting. Warp knitting uses several yarns and involves the interlocking of vertical loops with other loops on alternate sides. The result

is a fabric which does not ladder, unlike weft knitting. Both warp and weft knitting can be carried out industrially.

Braided fabrics tend to be used for heavy items such as carpets, mats, coats and jackets. They are formed by interweaving at least three yarns, but in a diagonal direction. The effect looks similar to plaiting.

Lace and net are examples of open-work fabrics. They consist of fine threads which are twisted around others at intervals to form an open structure. A pattern is formed by the holes created as well as by their positioning in the fabric.

A laminated fabric can be made by sticking or bonding two or more fabrics together. The fabrics may be laminated with a thin layer of foam, film or paper. Obviously this technique produces a firmer end-product than individual fabrics and may be used for protective coverings, such as wipeclean tablecloths.

▼ Examples of warp and weft knitting.

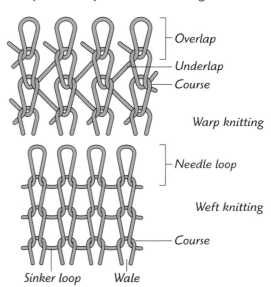

Overlap
Underlap
Course

Warp knitting

Needle loop

Weft knitting

Course

Sinker loop   Wale

35

testing fibres and fabrics

The success of a textile item may depend to a certain extent on the choice of fibre, or fibres, used to manufacture the fabric. 'Success' can be determined by the item's performance; put simply, if swimming trunks become see-through when wet they are unable to perform as successfully as you might want!

Consumer expectations of a textile item's performance will vary according to the product type. For instance, if you are buying an outfit for a special occasion, you may not worry about it being 'easy care' and accept that, on the few occasions you wear it, it will need to be dry cleaned. However, when you want an item such as a football shirt that gets a lot of use, its washability is likely to be a priority. Manufacturers will take the same sort of considerations into account when making products.

Testing times

To ensure fibres will perform in a certain way, tests can be carried out to determine their **properties**. It may also be a good idea to test fibres after they have been used in the production of a textile item. Ideally tests should be based on actual consumer use, but in reality it could take many years for some tests to be completed. Imagine testing the durability of a furnishing fabric used on a sofa or the effect of sunlight on a pair of curtains! Instead, textile technologists use sophisticated laboratory tests which, as far as possible, replicate what happens to the item during its 'life'.

When evaluating the **quality** of a product it is necessary to see which tests it has passed. The British Standards Institution (BSI) is a professional organization which decides on the tests to be carried out on different products and sets the standards that need to be applied. The textile industry is just one of many industries covered by British Standards.

The properties that can be tested in a laboratory include: durability, light fastness, flammability, shape retention, shrinkage, dye fastness, insulation, strength and water absorbancy.

Textile testing

All tests should meet the following requirements:

- As far as possible they must match what happens in real life.

- Reproducible results must be achieved; in other words, someone else can carry out the same test and get the same results.

- A specific measurement must be defined (a number or numeric value).

- Once results have been established, a measurement (or range of measurements) must be agreed as being acceptable to consumers.

Durability

Certain textile items such as carpets or suitcases must be very hard-wearing. Testing for durability is usually done by seeing how well a fabric stands up to abrasion (rubbing or grinding). The Martindale tester is an example of industrial machinery used to reproduce the 'wear and tear' of fabrics in controlled conditions. However, it is not just physical abrasion that can cause textile items to wear out. When subjected to sunlight, fibres weaken as the ultraviolet light attacks them, causing their **molecules** to break down. Chemicals found in perspiration and detergent also attack fibres over a period of time. Polyamides and polyester are particularly resistant to abrasion and chemical destruction; natural fibres are far less resilient.

Light fastness

Fabrics may be tested to see whether they will fade when exposed to sunlight. In order for the test to be carried out in a reasonable time, fabric is exposed to light that has the same characteristics of sunlight but at a much higher intensity. The fabric specimens are exposed alongside eight samples of standard dyed fabric with different light fastness. All samples are partly covered and it is the change between the exposed and covered parts of the specimen fabric compared with the change in the standard samples that determines the light fastness of the fabric.

Functional fabrics. Testing the performance of fabrics such as those used in the manufacture of tents is essential if consumers are to get satisfaction from their products. ▶

High-speed testing

Testing the functional characteristics of fabrics is very time consuming and trials can take as long as a year to complete. However, such tests are essential when the end-products are hot-air balloons, tents and paraglider canopies!

A recent development in the testing of fabrics for resilience to the elements is the QUV cabinet. This technology can produce reliable results in one week rather than over several months, by intensifying real-life weather conditions and so speeding up the ageing process. Fabrics can be subjected to simulations of outdoor conditions such as ultraviolet (UV) radiation, humidity and water spray, or combinations of these.

The tests can also be tailored for the specific end-use of the fabric, so tent fabrics for use in the UK would be put in conditions similar to the UK's climate: low levels of UV, cold temperatures and lots of rain!

taking care of fabrics

Most textile products carry care labels giving fibre content information, cleaning instructions and any other relevant information.

Caring for textiles

The **properties** of a fibre are obviously going to effect the way the end-product is cared for. If the fibres are blended, or the item contains more than one type of fabric, then the properties of all of them must be taken into consideration.

The cleaning of textile items doesn't necessarily involve washing them with water and detergent. A lamp shade may just require a brush or a wipe, while delicate items may have to be put through a special dry cleaning process. However, the following aspects of cleaning apply to items that need to be washed. They are considered by the manufacturer when washing labels are being prepared, and it is the fibre content that is taken into account. Of course, whether the washing labels are considered by the person who is about to squeeze a pile of dirty washing into the automatic machine is another matter!

1 Temperature of the water – Most cottons, for example, can be boiled, but if they have been coloured they may have to be washed at a lower temperature to prevent the dye from running.

2 Method of washing – Wool needs a very gentle washing action and often has to be washed by hand, whereas a polyester/cotton mix can cope with rougher treatment.

▲ A range of wash care labels.

3 Amount of water extraction – Most modern machines have different settings for spinning, so a gentle, short spin can be used for fibres such as acetate which crease badly.

4 Method of drying – Some fibres will shrink if tumble-dried, so a pair of trousers in polyester/viscose may have to be hung to dry naturally. Others may have to be drip-dried and not subjected to any wringing.

5 Type of ironing – Depending on their fibre composition, fabrics may or may not be ironed, and the temperature setting will vary. Linen fibres cope well with hot temperatures and, as they crease badly, this is important for smoothing out the fibres after washing. Certain acrylics, polyamides and polyesters can take only a cool iron because they are **thermoplastic** fibres, meaning they will soften and melt when subjected to a high temperature.

HLCC

To ensure that manufacturers use the same criteria when applying care labels to their textile items, the Home Laundering and Consultative Council has developed an International Textile Care Labelling Scheme. The scheme includes a set of symbols or codes to cover all aspects of laundering textile products. It is called the International Care Labelling Code and examples of its symbols and what they mean are shown on this page.

▼ *Laundering symbols. These have been devised by the HLCC and are found on many textile items.*

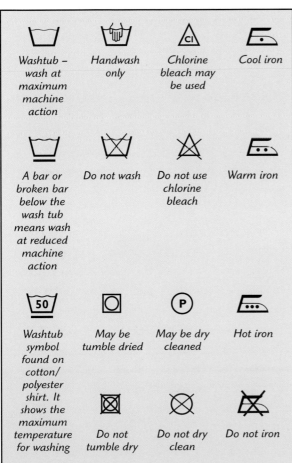

Washtub – wash at maximum machine action	Handwash only	Chlorine bleach may be used	Cool iron
A bar or broken bar below the wash tub means wash at reduced machine action	Do not wash	Do not use chlorine bleach	Warm iron
Washtub symbol found on cotton/ polyester shirt. It shows the maximum temperature for washing	May be tumble dried	May be dry cleaned	Hot iron
	Do not tumble dry	Do not dry clean	Do not iron

Additional labels

As well as providing care labels, on many textile items manufacturers are required by law to attach labels which give the consumer information about any risks from fire. Flammability warnings must appear on nightwear and upholstered furniture, and include expressions such as 'Carelessness causes fire', 'Warning – keep away from fire' or 'low flammability'. The British Standards Institution has set various standards of flammability which are recognized by a BSI number. These may be quoted on a label like this: 'Low Flammability to BS 5722'.

Quality labels

Finally, many items carry labels that show they are recognized by the British Standards Assurance Services. It is known as the kitemark, and tells the consumer that the item has been through regular routine testing during its production and therefore satisfies a particular standard.

▲ *The BSI kitemark shows that an item has been through regular routine testing during its production.*

innovative fabrics

Nylon was developed back in the 1930s, and although its use was limited to everyday items such as bristles for brushes, it soon found its way into the clothing industry. However, despite nylon's easy-care appeal and relatively low cost, consumers did not like its **aesthetic** qualities; it was functional, rather than comfortable.

One of nylon's main problems was its electrostatic charge. Nylon absorbs only small quantities of moisture, so when friction is created, perhaps by layers of clothing rubbing together, a charge occurs which can result in a crackling sound or even sparking. This friction was also the reason for clothes 'riding up'. For example, if in the 1950s a young woman went out wearing a nylon petticoat under a skirt with a nylon lining, the petticoat would gradually ride its way up to her waist. No wonder nylon clothes became unpopular!

So, it was up to the chemical company ICI to develop a new fibre that would have nylon's benefits without any of its disadvantages. Their market research suggested that the consumer demand was for comfort.

Tactel®

The fibre Tactel® was first launched in 1983 and was limited to the skiwear market. Within two years Tactel® had secured 50% of this market.

The fibre is made from a high-quality polyamide, and combines the strength of nylon with the softer **qualities** of natural fibres. The name Tactel® actually comes from the Latin *tacto* ('I touch'), which implies softness, but the fabric is also very lightweight. Tactel® **yarns** are 30% lighter than cotton or polyester and have the highest 'strength-to-weight' ratio of any fibre.

It is easy to see how Tactel® moved swiftly from being a big hit in skiwear to an equivalent success in the clothing industry. It could produce highly fashionable garments out of highly functional fabrics. A whole range of yarns and fabrics was developed to produce all kinds of clothing – from hard-wearing, functional, outdoor garments to soft, luxurious lingerie.

Tactel® is used to produce a whole range of clothes that are both fashionable and functional. ▶

There are a variety of Tactel® fibres which have specific qualities and characteristics.

Tactel® Micro

Tactel® Micro is an extremely fine fibre, 60 times finer than a strand of human hair! However, as it is a polyamide it is also very strong, so it is used in the production of lingerie and hosiery (stockings, tights, socks etc).

Tactel® Aquator

Tactel® Aquator is used for sportswear and functional underwear. As its name suggests, its job is to keep moisture away from the skin. It actually provides the garment with an inner layer, as you can see in the diagram. This inner layer is able to transfer moisture away from the body towards the outer layer of the clothing, so keeping the skin dry. The moisture can then evaporate away more easily, which increases a person's comfort.

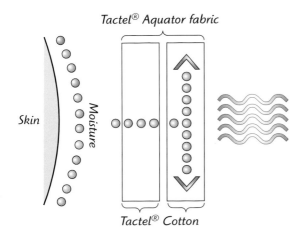

▲ How Tactel® Aquator fabric works. Moisture is drawn away from the body towards the outer layer of the fabric.

An example of Tactel® Aquator being put to use can be seen in the following promotional material from MAXIT Fabrics:

'Cotton Wick is a different type of MAXIT fabric that draws moisture to the outside ... keeping you dry on the inside. The fabric is based on a unique two-layered construction. The inner layer of Tactel fibers **wicks** moisture from the body to the outer cotton layer. The moisture is then dispersed over a large surface area away from the skin where it evaporates, keeping the wearer dry and comfortable.'

Tactel® Diabolo

The third type of Tactel® is Diabolo, which provides many of the aesthetic qualities that were lacking in nylon. This fibre provides fabrics with a wonderful lustre and soft handle. They **drape** beautifully, and consequently have been used extensively in the production of lingerie, as well as sportswear.

DuPont takeover

In 1993 DuPont acquired ICI fibres' worldwide nylon businesses, including Tactel®, which is why it is now a registered trademark of DuPont.

However, Dupont constantly researches and develops new ideas in order to improve the functional and aesthetic qualities of textile fibres.

fabric developments

As we have seen, **cellulose** is the starting point for natural cotton fibres and regenerated fibres such as viscose.

A recent development in fabrics using cellulosic fibres has been the creation of Tencel®, which is the brand name for a fibre made using wood pulp from trees grown on special farms in the USA. It took many years to develop, and actually belongs to an innovative **generic** class of fibres called lyocell.

Save the trees

Lyocell developed out of a desire to produce a more ecologically sound fibre – one which was both biodegradable and non-toxic to the environment. First, the wood pulp had to come from 'managed forests', where trees were constantly being replanted. Second, the process should not create any toxic chemical products which could be released into the atmosphere. From an industrial point of view, it is cheaper to avoid waste than to have to recycle it.

Market research has also shown that although consumers appreciate the functional **qualities** of manufactured fibres they still prefer the **aesthetic** qualities of natural fibres. So, a new way of producing fibres had to be found that was both environmentally friendly and resulted in an easy-care fibre with a natural look and feel.

Revolutionary spinning

Many years of research resulted in a revolutionary new spinning process called solvent spinning. It involved dissolving cellulose (from wood pulp) in a solution of water, cellulose and a substance called NMMO (an amineoxide). The bonus of this process is that it does not result in any chemical reaction. The spinning solution is then filtered and spun by means of **spinnerets** into a 'coagulation bath' containing pure water. Finally, as much of the NMMO solvent as possible is recovered, usually 97%. This is not because it is harmful but because it is expensive. So, in terms of profits, it is better to recycle as much as possible. The remaining thread is then washed, dried and put on to bobbins for further processing.

▼ The environmentally friendly production of lyocell.

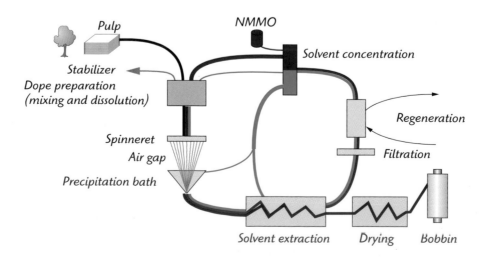

What are its characteristics?

Tencel® has the characteristics of a luxury fibre yet it is very strong. It is naturally absorbant which makes it comfortable to wear, and it readily accepts dye. It is washable, resists creases and does not shrink. The spinning process for Tencel® results in round filament fibres with a smooth surface, but the fabric can have either a bright **lustre** or a matt finish. Best of all, it has a luxurious look and feel, so it **drapes** beautifully.

How does it compare?

In terms of strength, Tencel® compares well with any manufactured fibre. It is as comfortable as cotton and has the depth of colour that can be achieved with viscose fibres. It has qualities similar to silk, in that it is aesthetically pleasing and soft to the touch.

Will it blend?

Tencel® can be blended with other fibres to produce a fabric with enhanced qualities. For instance, it can be combined with linen, Lycra®, cotton and very fine polyesters. As it is strong, Tencel® can produce very fine, soft fabrics that do not crease easily.

Courtaulds trademark

In 1992, after many years of development of lyocell fibres, Courtaulds launched Tencel®, their particular brand of lyocell. It is the registered trademark used by Courtaulds for their apparel textile items.

Courtaulds have continued to develop other uses for lyocell fibres outside the clothing industry. The fibres are suitable for other 'breathable' fabric items – for example, tents, outdoor clothing and overalls. When produced as non-woven fabrics they can also be used for medicinal purposes, such as dressings and hygiene wipes.

▼ *Tencel® is a popular fibre for clothes because it is comfortable and hard-wearing, with a luxurious look and feel.*

Books

The following books are useful for students studying GCSE Design and Technology: Textiles Technology.

Design & Make It! Textiles Technology Alex McArthur, Carolyn Etchells, Tristram Shepard	Stanley Thornes 1997
Examining Textiles Technology Anne Barnett	Heinemann Educational 1997
Textiles and Technology (UK edition) Adapted by Margaret Beith	Cambridge University Press 1997
Textiles Technology Alison Bartle and Bernie O'Connor	Causeway Press 1997

The following books are useful for more detailed fibre information.

The Motivate Series: Textiles Andrea Wynne	Macmillan Education 1997
Textiles Properties and Behaviour in Clothing Use Edward Miller	B T Batsford Ltd 1992

I.C.T.

www.craftscouncil.org.uk/exhib.htm
Provides details of forthcoming arts and crafts events throughout the country

www.ecotex.com/faq.htm
Lists frequently asked questions (and answers) about Tencel®

www.textile-toolkit.org.uk
Includes news, competitions, details of events and a chat forum for students. There is also a CD-ROM available for use as a teaching aid for GCSE textiles

www.worldtextile.com
The website of World Textile Publications, publishers of Textile Horizons (Perkin House, 1 Longlands Street, Bradford BD1 2TP)

Places to visit

Quarry Bank Mill, Styal, Cheshire
Built as a cotton spinning and weaving mill in 1784 by Samuel Greg, this is now a working museum of the British Cotton Industry

Victoria and Albert Museum
Cromwell Road
South Kensington
London SW7 2RL
(Tel no: 020 7942 2000)
Textile exhibitions and Crafts Council shop

Syon Park, London
(Tel no: 020 8560 0881)
Arts and crafts events and shows throughout the year, an arts centre and needlecraft centre as well as house and gardens to visit

Island Heritage
Pott Hill Farm
Near Leighton Reservoir
Healey, Masham
North Yorkshire HG4 4LT
(Tel no: 01765 689651)
A working Dales farm, producing natural, undyed woollen products from rare-breed, primitive sheep

The Crafts Study Centre
Holburne Museum
Great Pulteney Street
Bath BA2 4DB
(Tel no: 01225 466669)
The Centre's collection includes ceramics, printed and woven textiles, furniture and calligraphy

Contacts

The Crafts Council
44a Pentonville Road
London NI 9BY
(Tel no: 020 7278 7700)
Provides up-to-date information about art and crafts exhibitions and shows; also produces a magazine called Crafts, available on subscription

glossary

aesthetic relates to the beauty of something rather than other considerations

affinities where things have a close similarity or connection

amino acids organic compounds

bale large bundle of fibres (such as cotton) that have been bound together

cellulose the main substance in plant cell walls

continuous filaments long fibres that are produced naturally or manufactured in one length

crimp the waviness of a fibre

drape the way in which a fabric hangs

dry spinning a method of spinning manufactured fibres which uses warm air and solvent

durable long lasting, hard-wearing

ecologically sound where something is grown with due consideration to the environment

extensibility the ability of a fibre to extend without breaking

fibrils tiny fibres

fleece sheep's wool

generic group or class

glucose sugar in its natural form; a source of energy made and used by plants and animals

Industrial Revolution the development of technological advances in Britain

interliner (also called interfacing) fabric placed in between two layers of fabric to strengthen the item (e.g. at the cuffs, waistband and collar of clothing)

labour-intensive involving a lot of work and taking a lot of time

lustre shine or gloss

melt spinning a method of spinning manufactured fibres in which the polymer is melted and forced through a spinneret, after which it cools and sets in the form of a filament

molecule small unit of matter, made up of two or more atoms joined together

monomer chemical compound made up of simple molecules, from which polymers can be made

photosynthesis a process used by plants to make cellulose from carbon dioxide and water using the light energy absorbed by their chlorophyll

polymer a natural or synthetic compound that has large molecules made from simple units called monomers

polymerization the process of making polymers

properties qualities or characteristics of a fabric, e.g 'durable'

quality a high degree or level of excellence

selvedge a firm area of fabric created by strong warp threads being placed along the edge of the fabric

spinneret device used in the production of manufactured fibres; it contains very fine holes through which liquid is forced

spinning a process of twisting fibres together to produce yarns

staple fibres relatively short fibres (up to about 25cm), compared with the long fibres of continuous filaments

tactile relating to the sense of touch or how something feels

tenacity the strength of a fibre

tensile strength the strength of a fibre

thermoplastic becoming soft when heated and hard again once cooled

viscous having a thick consistency

warp the vertical threads in a woven fabric

weft the horizontal threads in a woven fabric

wet spinning a method of spinning manufactured fibres using a bath of chemicals

wicks the way moisture runs along a fibre even if the fibre is completely non-absorbant

worsted fine, firm, smooth yarn that has been spun from long strands of wool with a high degree of twist

yarn single strand consisting of fibres that have been spun together

index